Zion National Park's south entrance monument was built with native stone by the Civilian Conservation Corps in 1935.

Zion National Park

Photographers – Dan Blackburn, Tim Fitzharris, Howie Garber, John P. Goerge, Robert Hildebrand, Dai Hirota, Liz Hymans, Tom & Pat Leeson, David Muench, Marc Muench, William Neill/Larry Ulrich Photography, Carol Polich, Bill Proud, Larry Ulrich, John Wagner, and Jamie & Judy Wild

ISBN-13 978-1-60068-156-1

First Printing, May, 2008

4961 Windplay Drive, El Dorado Hills, CA 95762
www.impactphotographics.com

Printed in China

Massive cliffs of Navajo Sandstone towering more than 2,000 feet above the canyon floor define the character of Zion National Park.

Sunset illuminates the Watchman near the south entrance to Zion National Park.

The Springdale Member of the Moenave Formation forms a solid foundation for these cliffs of Kayenta and Navajo Sandstone at the mouth of Zion Canyon.

The Watchman guards the south entrance to Zion Canyon in this evening view from the Pa'rus Trail.

Morning light creeps up on the massive Temples and Towers of the Virgin standing against the western skyline of Zion National Park.

The tops of cottonwood and box elder trees form a verdant canopy over the Virgin River beneath Zion Canyon's ever-present towers of stone.

The southward view from the mouth of Zion Canyon takes in Johnson Mountain on the left and the Eagle Crags on the center horizon.

The elegant arch of Pine Creek Bridge, at the foot of the switchbacks leading up to the Zion-Mt. Carmel Tunnel, frames Zion's West Temple on the center horizon.

The West Temple of Zion is one of the park's iconic landmarks, a near-symmetrical tower visible from many miles to the east and west.

Cactus blooms on the floor of Zion Canyon add a special accent to a scene already saturated with the characteristic colors of the Navajo Sandstone.

The pinnacle of the perfectly named Angels Landing can be reached along a strenuous 2.5-mile trail, an exhilarating hike for those who are not afraid of heights.

In 1916, the Methodist minister Frederick Vining Fisher, along with his local guide Claud Hirschi, named the Three Patriarchs: Abraham, Isaac, and Jacob.

Abraham and Isaac, two of the pinnacles in Zion National Park's Court of the Patriarchs, stand watch over a snow-dusted winter wonderland.

Magical waterfalls stream from hidden canyons during spring runoff and after summer rains in Zion Canyon.

Cascading water in the creeks feeding into the Virgin River contribute to the perennial flow that has carved Zion Canyon through eons of time.

Golden box elder and cottonwood trees line the banks of the Virgin River adding to the autumn splendor of Zion National Park.

The original Zion Lodge, built in the 1920s, was destroyed by fire and quickly rebuilt in 1966. In 1992, a reconstruction restored much of the lodge's original character.

A constant dripping spring emerges from the porous Navajo Sandstone and feeds the hanging gardens of ferns and mosses at Weeping Rock.

Zion National Park is home to 68 species of mammals, including mountain lion, desert bighorn sheep, and prairie dog.

Zion National Park's Great White Throne, seen here from an unusually high vantage, is one of the Canyon's most photographed landmarks.

The Virgin River gently winds its way down the canyon it has carved during millions of years of erosion.

The switchback section known as Walter's Wiggles on the West Rim Trail to Angels Landing was built under the direction of the park's first acting superintendent, Walter Reusch.

Upon naming the Great White Throne in 1916, the Methodist minister Frederick Vining Fisher said,
"It is by all odds America's masterpiece."

The rocks have no monopoly on color in Zion Canyon as a wide variety of wildflowers abound, including Indian paintbrush, claret cup cactus, and desert phlox.

The Pulpit, at the Temple of Sinawava, can be seen from the last shuttle stop at the north end of the Zion Canyon Scenic Drive.

The Virgin River has cut a remarkable slender chasm through the Navajo Sandstone in the northern part of Zion Canyon known as The Narrows.

Water miraculously seeps from sandstone creating magnificent hanging gardens along the face of Zion Canyon.

Though quiet and serene most days, the Virgin River can swell to a raging torrent after heavy rainfall, as evidenced by the chaotic erosion in the Zion Narrows.

The year-round march of water to lower ground creates some of the most idyllic settings in Zion National Park, including this scene in the Left Fork of North Creek.

The perspective from Canyon Overlook Trail offers an excellent view of the switchback road leading up Pine Creek Canyon to the mile-long Zion-Mt. Carmel Tunnel.

This angle from Canyon Overlook Trail offers examples of ancient crossbedding in the Navajo Sandstone, with the Towers of the Virgin on the western horizon.

Built in the late 1920s, the mile-long Zion-Mt. Carmel Tunnel is one of Zion National Park's most astounding man-made wonders.

Water, wind, and time have created a variety of shapes and designs in Zion, many of which are intimately accessible on the park's east side.

The honeycomb effect seen in many of the rocks of Zion National Park is the result of weathering in the Navajo Sandstone.

A small but shapely ponderosa pine clings to a ledge of Navajo Sandstone in Zion National Park's Clear Creek Canyon.

Kolob Canyons

Lava Point

Zion Narrows

Temple of Sinawava

Angels Landing

Weeping Ro

Runoff from Cedar Mountain on the Markagunt Plateau (on the horizon) has carved the magnificent maze of canyons now comprised in Zion National Park.

Canyon Junction

Great Arch of Zion

Zion Lodge

Bridge Mountian

Checkerboard Mesa

The Zion-Mt. Carmel Highway climbs through the east side of Zion National Park past the Great Arch of Zion, through the mile-long tunnel, and along the base of Checkerboard Mesa.

Checkerboard Mesa, on Zion National Park's east side, is a textbook example of horizontal and vertical joints in Navajo Sandstone.

The textures of Zion are found not only in the variety of shapes in the crossbedded sandstone, but also in the array of plants and trees that grow in the park.

Surreal evening light transforms a landscape into a dreamscape along Zion National Park's Kolob Terrace.

The deep green needles of pine trees are given texture and heightened color by the red Navajo Sandstone at Double Arch Alcove and Kolob Arch in the Kolob Canyons section of Zion.

At sunset the great cliffs of Kolob Canyons seem to catch fire as the sun's dying rays infuse the rocks with deep vermillion hues.

Simple creeks have carved the high mesas and deep drainages found in Zion National Park's Kolob Canyons.

Extreme weathering has led to the many shapes and hues found in the rocks and hoodoos at Cedar Breaks National Monument.

At 10,000 feet above sea level, Cedar Breaks National Monument marks the spot where a pine-studded forest breaks into an amphitheater of vermillion spires, pinnacles and knife-edged ledges.

Verdant summertime meadows covered with a delightful array of wildflowers flow to the dramatic drop-off of Cedar Breaks National Monument.